ABCDE-F YOU

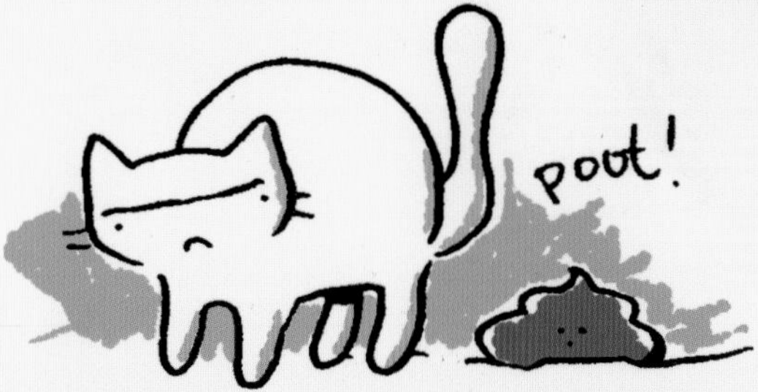
poot!

STERLING
New York

An Imprint of Sterling Publishing
1166 Avenue of the Americas
New York, NY 10036

ISBN 978-1-4549-1720-5

Distributed in Canada by Sterling Publishing
℅ Canadian Manda Group, 664 Annette Street
Toronto, Ontario, Canada M6S 2C8
Distributed in the United Kingdom by GMC Distribution Services
Castle Place, 166 High Street, Lewes, East Sussex, England BN7 1XU
Distributed in Australia by Capricorn Link (Australia) Pty. Ltd.
P.O. Box 704, Windsor, NSW 2756, Australia

For information about custom editions, special sales, and premium and corporate purchases, please contact Sterling Special Sales at 800-805-5489 or specialsales@sterlingpublishing.com.

Manufactured in China

2 4 6 8 10 9 7 5 3 1

www.sterlingpublishing.com

ABCDE·F·YOU

the abc's of cat ownership

by katie cook

STERLING
New York

A is for ass. Your cat will lick his own vigorously and loudly at all times. Really. It'll sound like he's eating ribs in the next room.

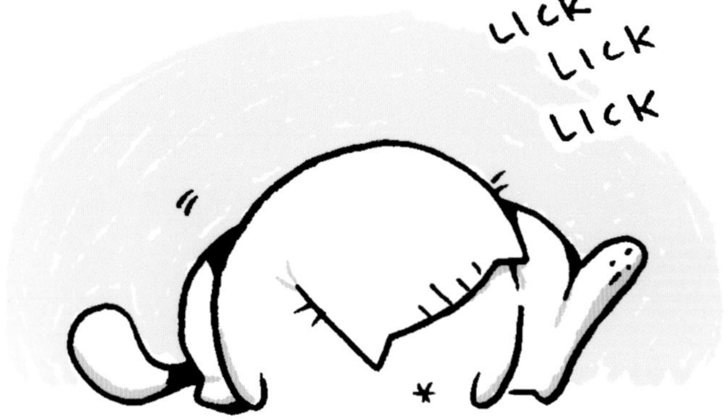
LICK
LICK
LICK

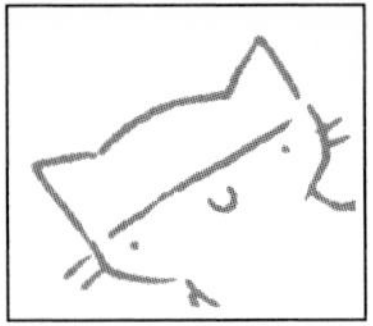

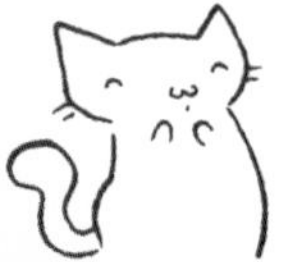

B is for bored. Your cat is easily bored. You will buy your cat lots of expensive cat toys, scratching posts, and catnip treats. Your cat will want the plastic ring off a milk jug over all those things.

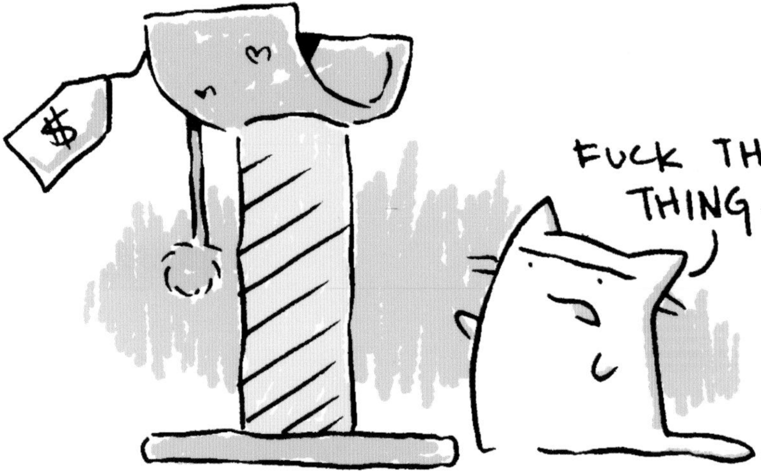
$
FUCK THAT THING.

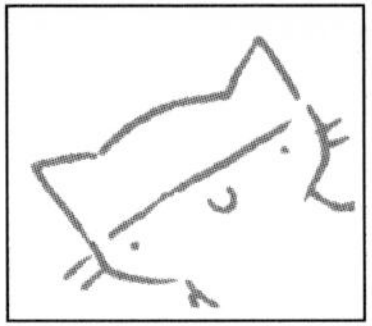

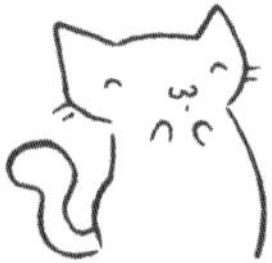

C is for callous. Callous is defined as "having an insensitive and cruel disregard for others." Otherwise defined as "a cat."

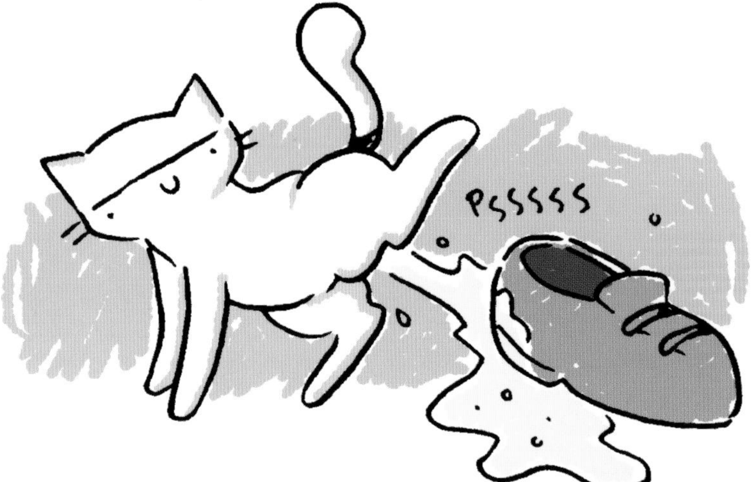
PSSSSS

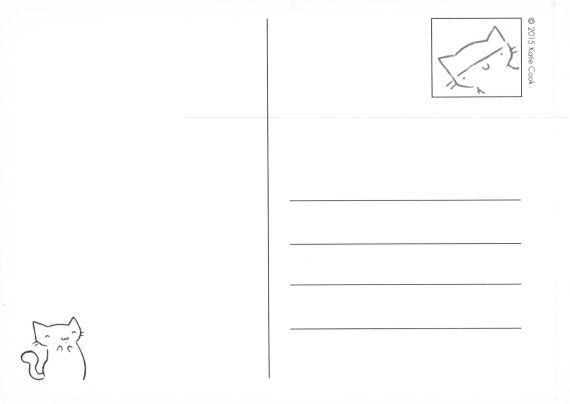

D is for dysfunctional. This is the defining characteristic of all relationships between a cat and the rest of the world.

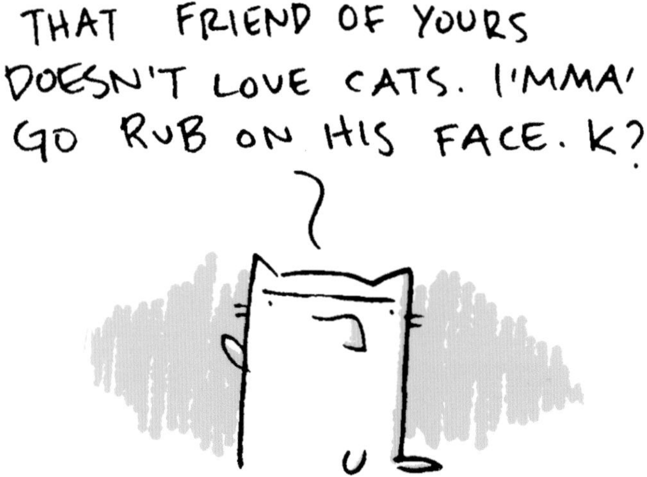
THAT FRIEND OF YOURS DOESN'T LOVE CATS. I'MMA' GO RUB ON HIS FACE. K?

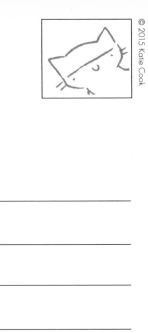

E is for everything you own, which is covered in hair. Thin, pointy hair that penetrates and adheres to every fabric, creates hair tumbleweeds on hardwood floors, and is impossible to rid yourself of. Don't even try to. Give up now.

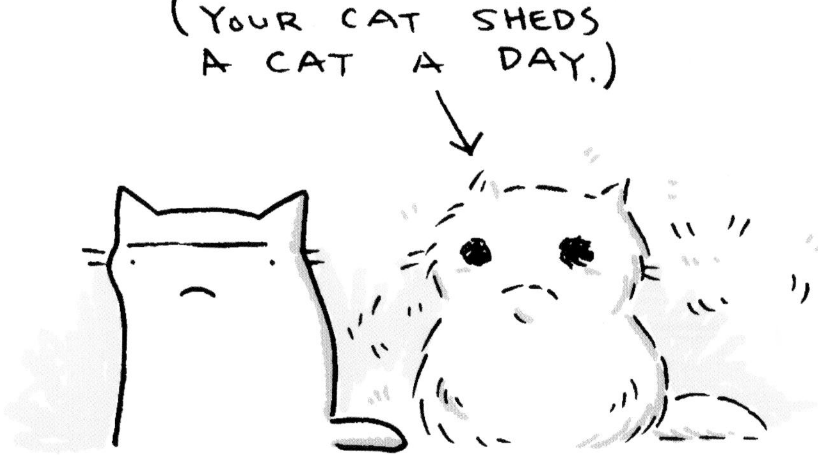
(YOUR CAT SHEDS A CAT A DAY.)

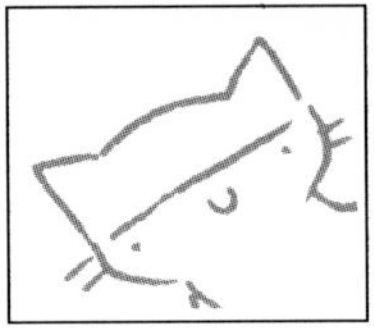

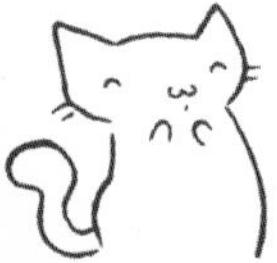

F is for fussy damn fuss bucket. Your cat will be pickier than any toddler about the food it eats and when it deems you worthy of petting it. F is also for "fuck off," which your cat wants you to do 90% of the time.

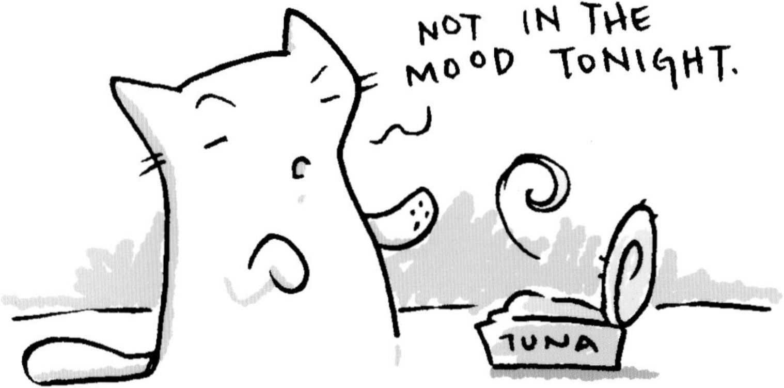
NOT IN THE MOOD TONIGHT.
TUNA

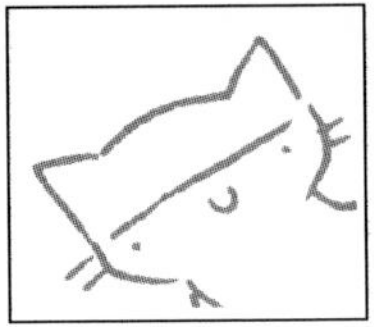

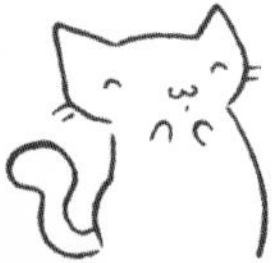

G is for godlike. In ancient Egypt, cats were worshiped as gods. Do you think they've forgotten this? No, they haven't.

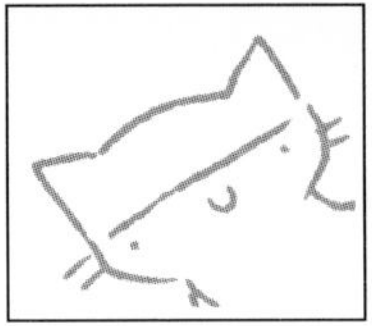

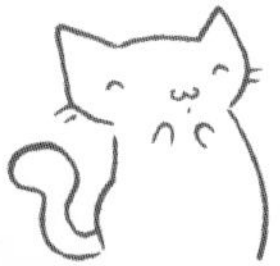

H is for your own personal hell. You got the cat. You brought this on yourself. (H can also stand for hateful, headstrong, hostile, hissing, and heartless . . . because I like alliteration.)

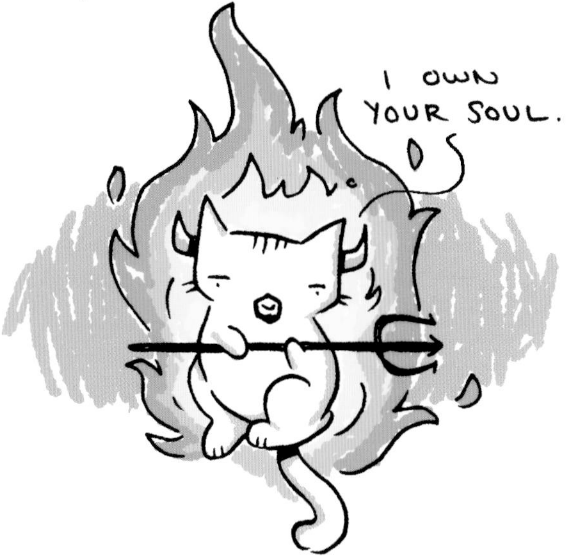
I OWN
YOUR SOUL.

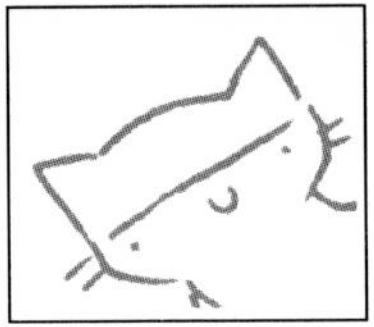

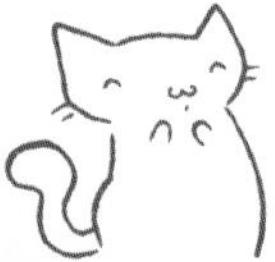

I is for irrational. Having a cat is like dating a 17-year-old high school girl. Stepping on its tail will be seen as breaking up with her at prom. Everything you do will be taken out of context and lorded over you until one of you DIES.

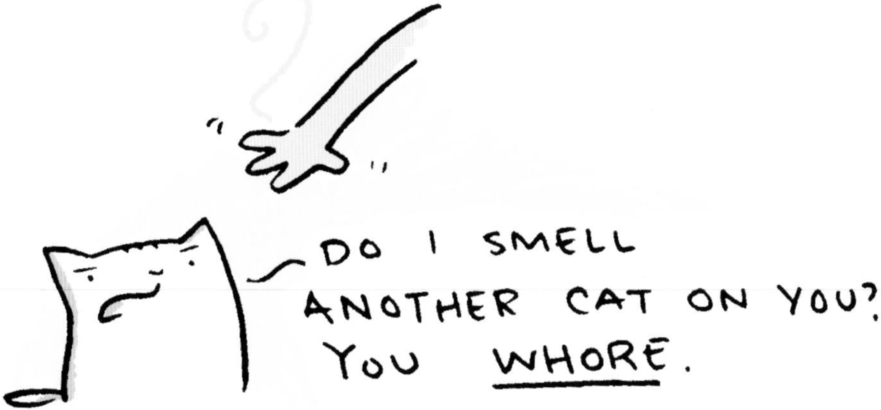
DO I SMELL ANOTHER CAT ON YOU? YOU WHORE.

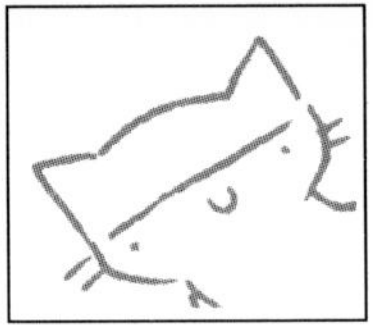

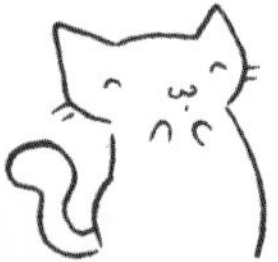

J is for jittery. Cats, when awake, will act like they've just consumed 37 cups of coffee. They will meow at the wall when there is nothing there. They will take off in a dead run for no reason. They are either paranoid or can see ghosts.

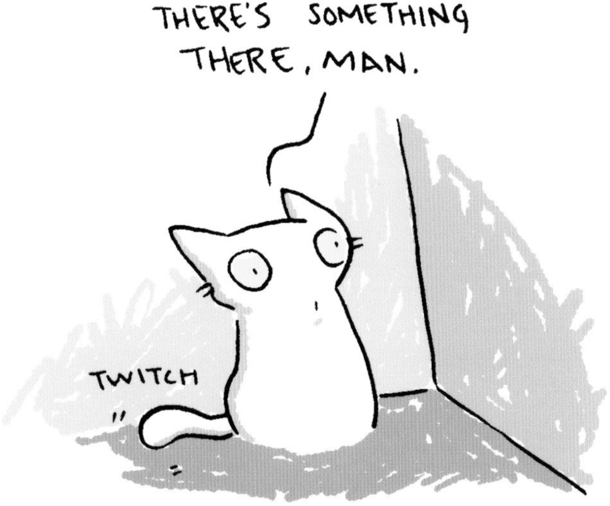
THERE'S SOMETHING THERE, MAN.
TWITCH

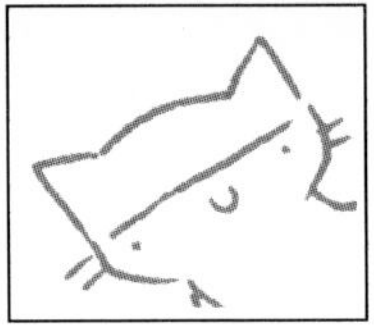

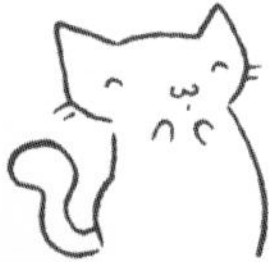

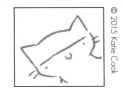

K is for kindness . . . which your cat shows on rare occasion to deepen your suffering from Stockholm Syndrome.

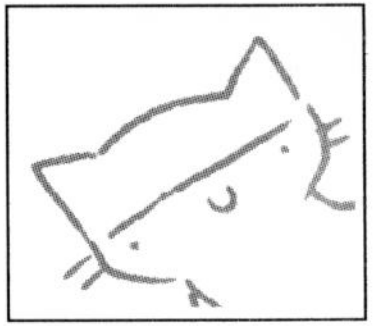

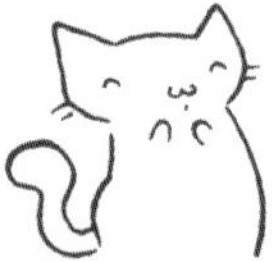

L is for licking. SO. MUCH. DAMN. LICKING. This is supposedly done for "cleaning," but it is really done to create hairballs that are thrown up where you tend to step when you are not paying attention.

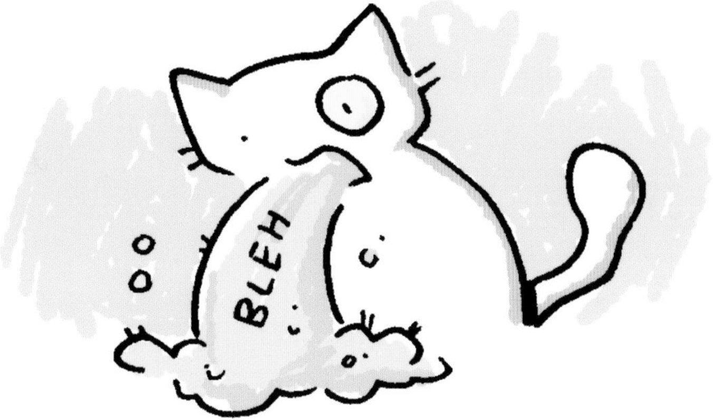
BLEH

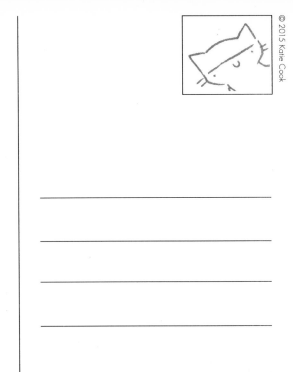

M is for morbid. Your cat thinks bug carcasses and dead mice are a suitable gift to bring you. Check your pillow at night before you go to bed—an "offering" may have been left. Bleh.

I WORKED ALL DAY TO BRING YOU THIS DEAD SQUIRREL. YOU BETTER FUCKING LOVE IT.

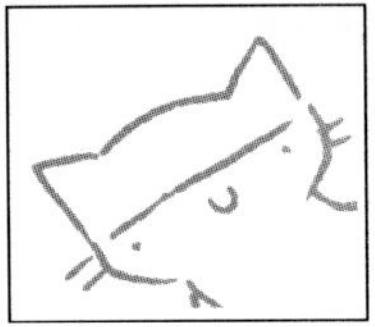

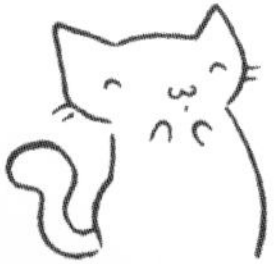

N is for narcoleptic, which explains a lot about cats. A cat can fall asleep in any place at any time and in any pose.

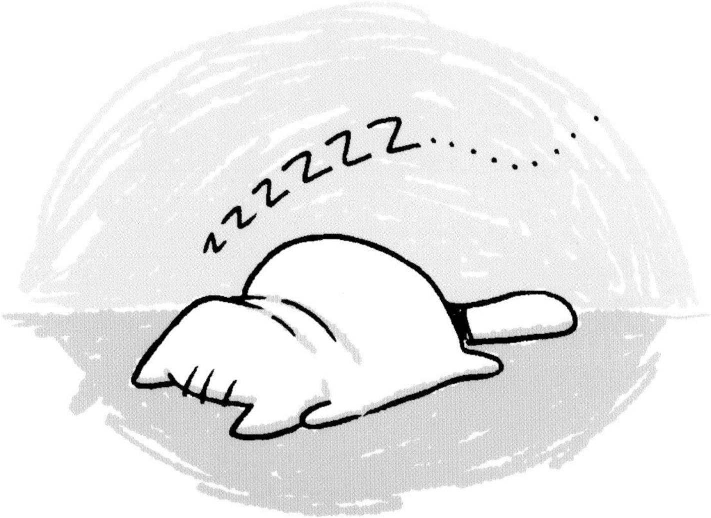
zzzzzzZ.........

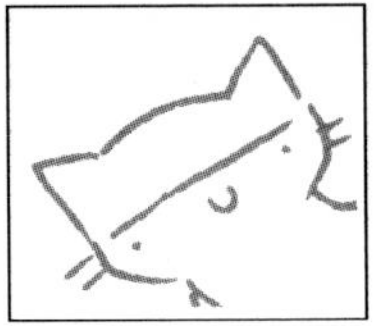

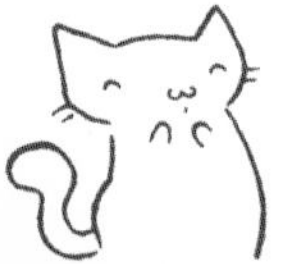

O is for obedient . . . If you wanted this to be part of the deal, you should have gotten a dog.

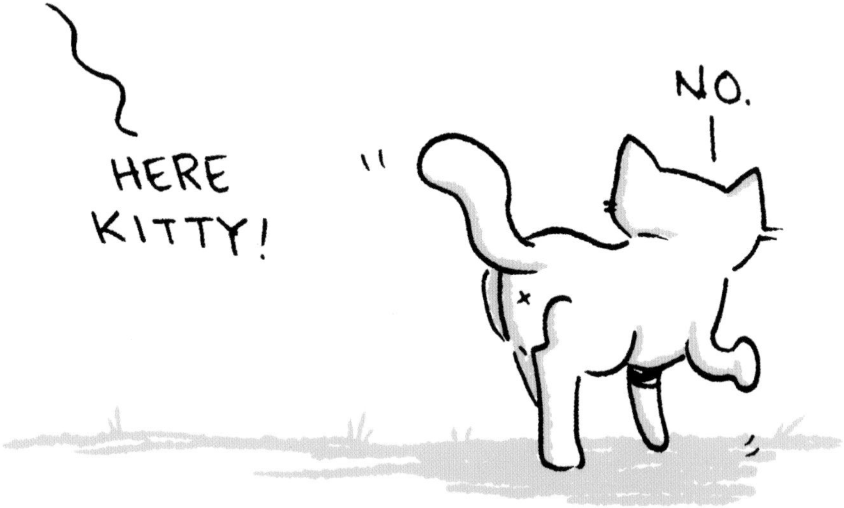
HERE KITTY!
NO.

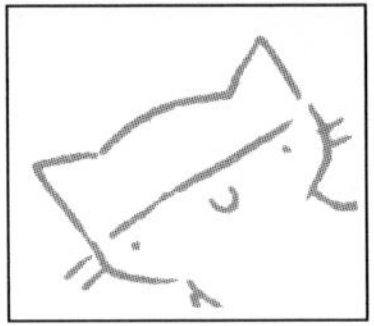

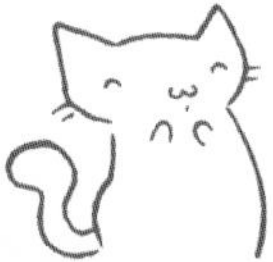

P is for pussy. (He-he!)

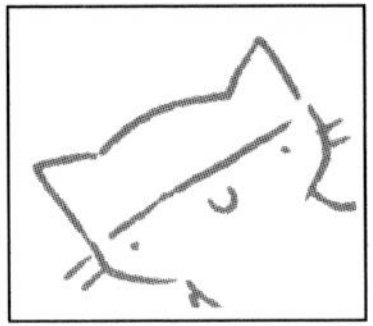

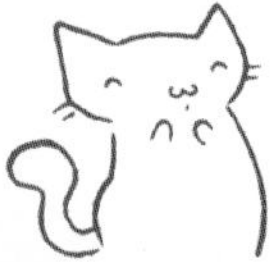

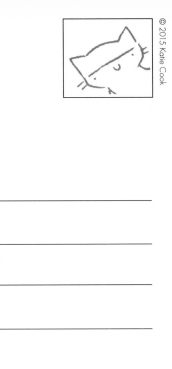

Q is for queen? Quadrifoliate? Quail? I don't know. This one is hard.

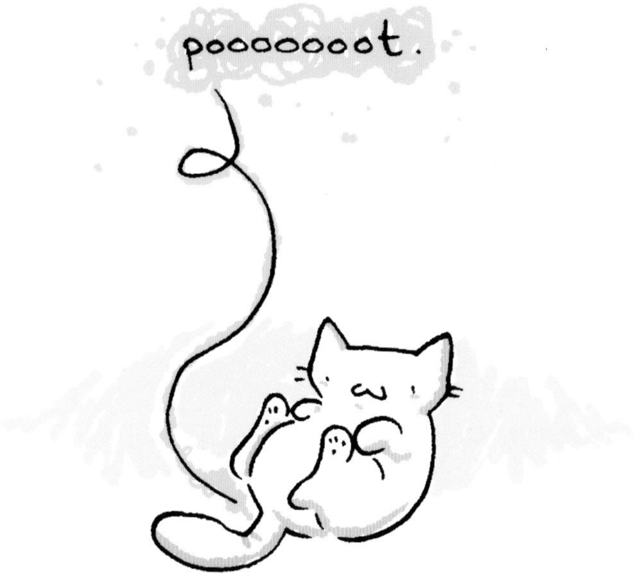
poooooooot.

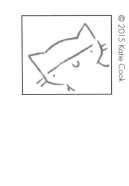

R is for reckless. Cats are not careful about . . . well, anything. Your cat will attempt parkour around your living room with no thought to what clinging to your curtains for dear life will do to those $39.99 drapes from Target.

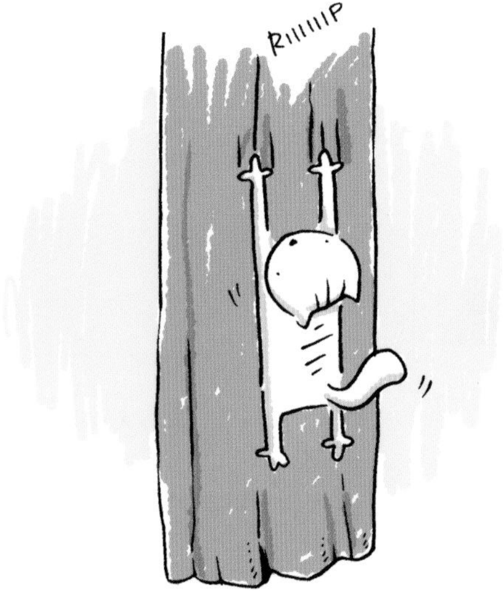
RIIIIIIP

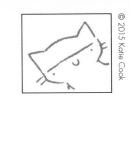

S is for shit, which your cat does in a box that YOU have to clean . . . daily. Let us not forget those lovely times when your cat will decide that box is for SUCKERS and decide not to use it.

COME CLEAN UP
MY SHIT.

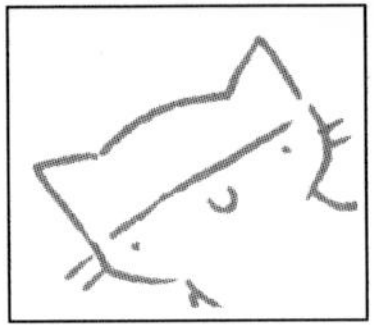

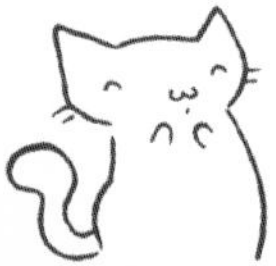

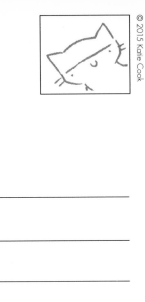

T is for thankless. See "cat ownership."

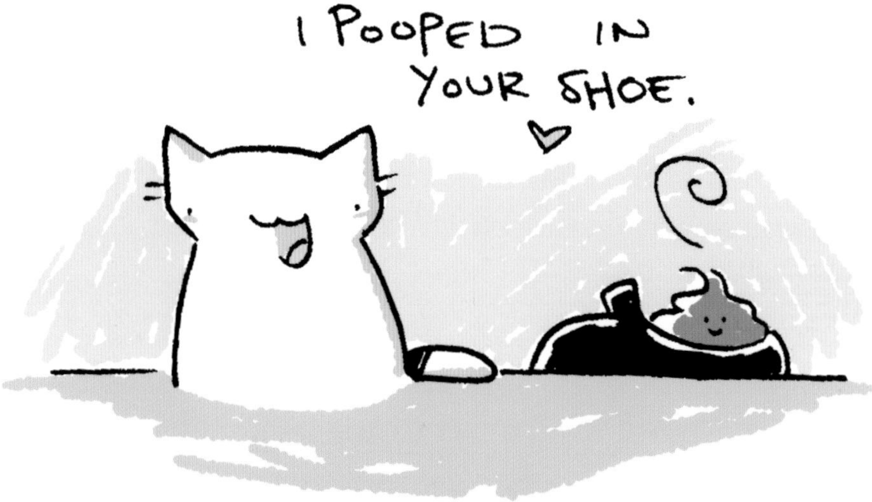
I POOPED IN YOUR SHOE.

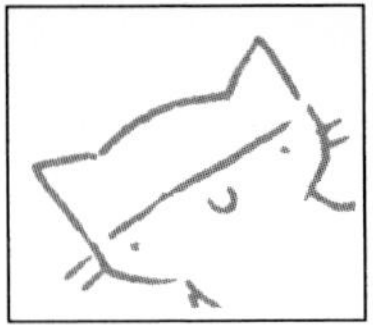

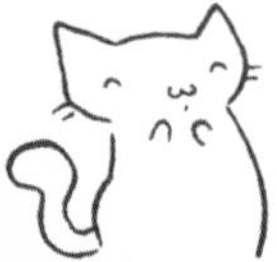

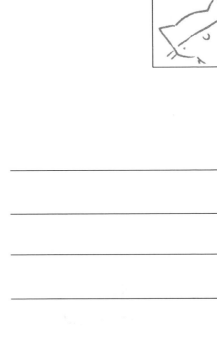

U is for urine. Smelly, awful cat urine. Your house is now 100% permeated by this smell and it will never ever ever go away. You will begin to adjust, but every non-cat owner who visits you will notice it and be too polite to say anything.

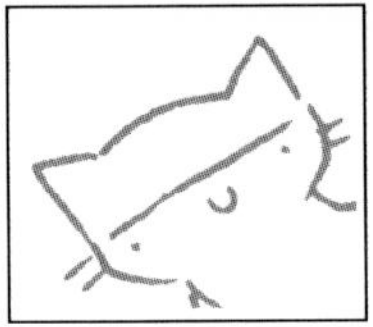

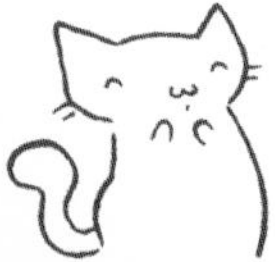

V is for vulnerable, which all your worldly possessions now are. Every piece of clothing will get a claw hole, knickknacks will be strewn off shelves, and water glasses will be spilled onto your iPhone 5 (probably on purpose).

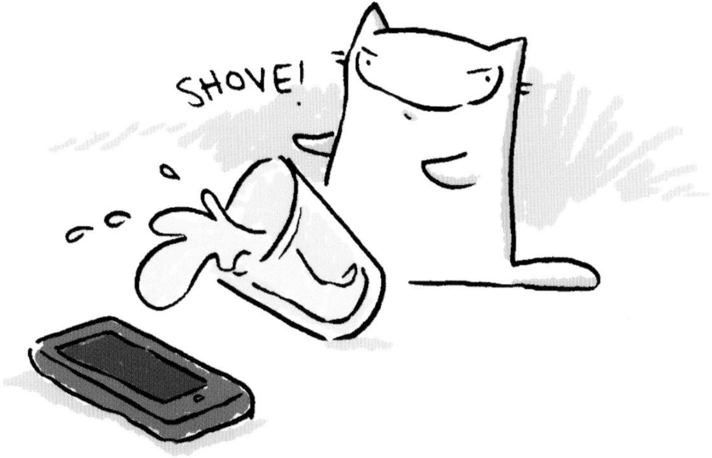
SHOVE!

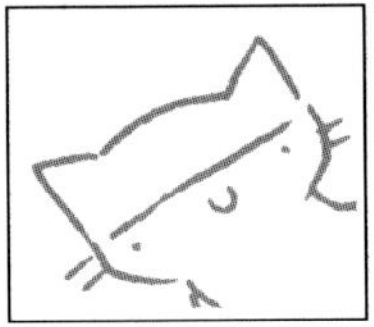

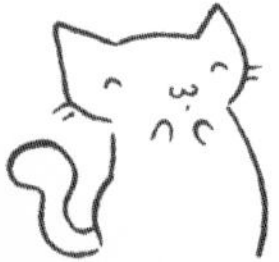

W is for worrisome. If you own a cat and you haven't heard a meow or crash in 20 minutes, be concerned. That cat is up to something.

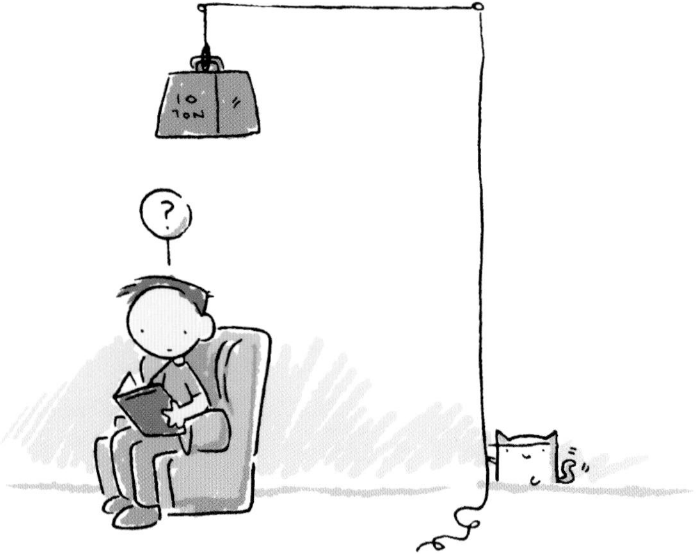
10
TON
?

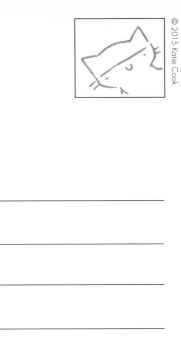

X is for the shape of those fresh scratches all over your arm.

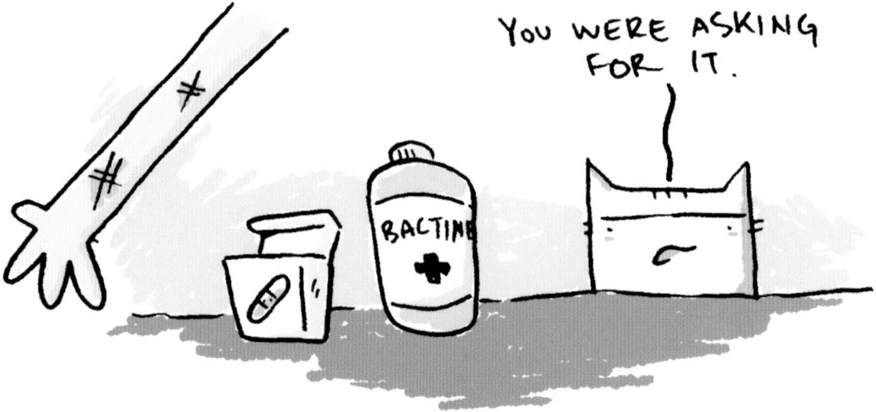
YOU WERE ASKING FOR IT.
BACTINE

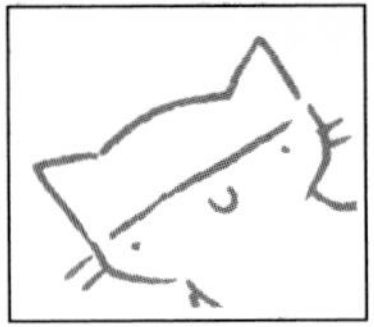

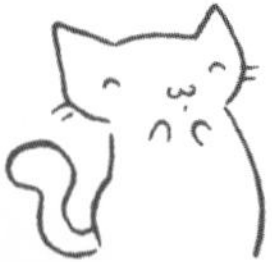

Y is for yearning to own a dog instead. You know, a sweet, obedient, loving dog that would protect your body instead of eating your corpse, should you fall down dead in your own home.

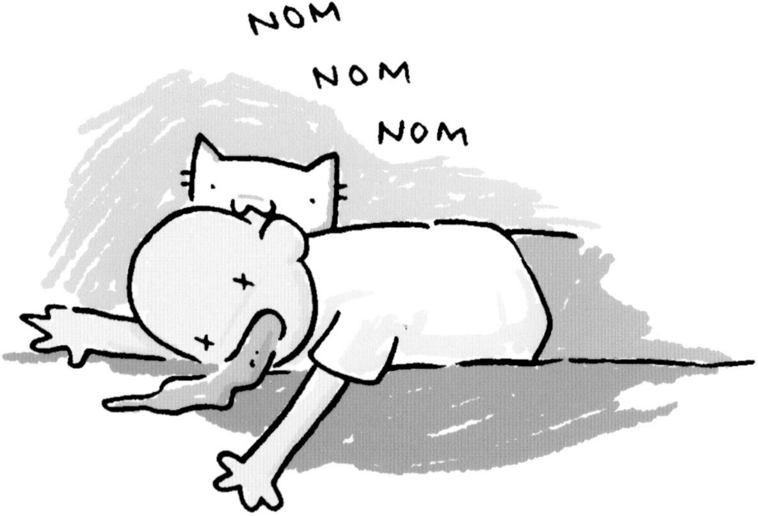
NOM
NOM
NOM

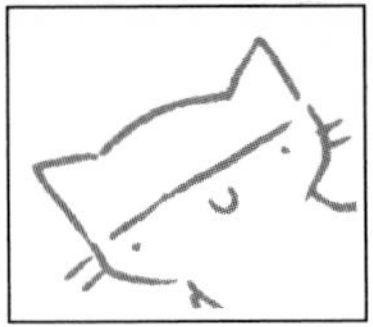

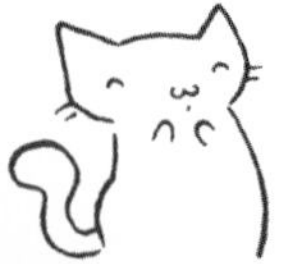

Z is for zen, which cat ownership provides 4% of the time . . . and that 4% makes the other 96% of the time totally worthwhile.

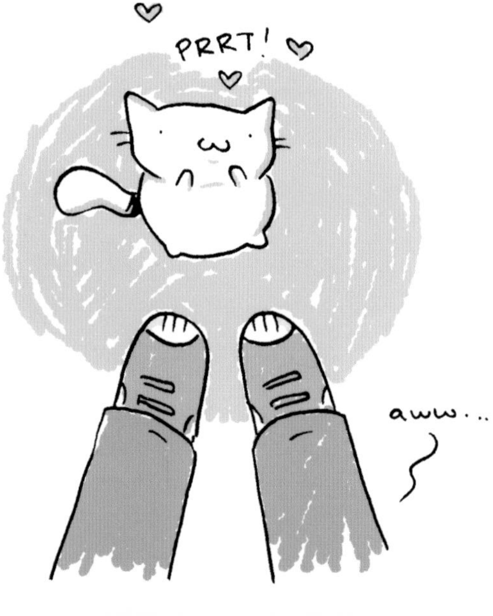

PRRT!
aww...

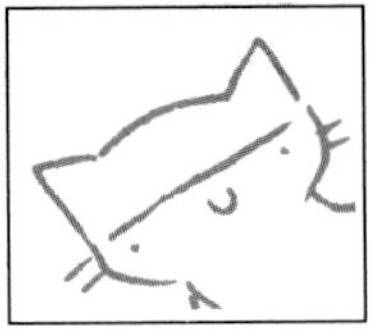

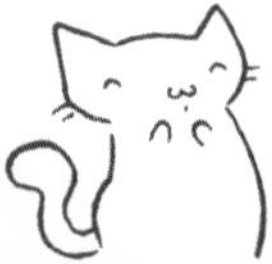

THE END.

For iPod, Lupin, and Oscar . . . my favorite furry little bastards.

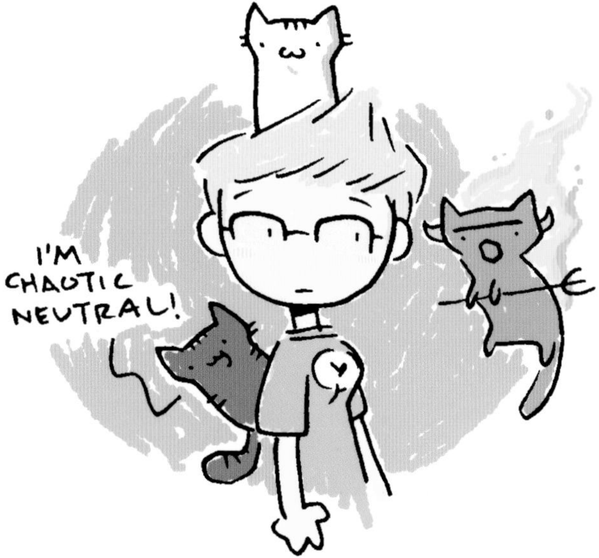
I'M CHAOTIC NEUTRAL!

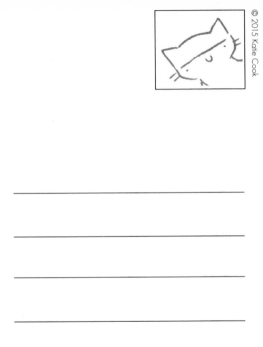

poooooot.

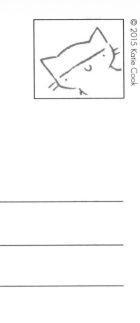

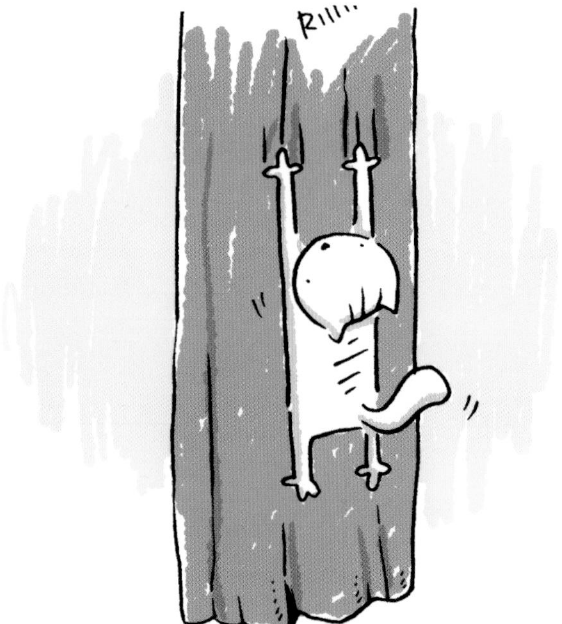
RIII...

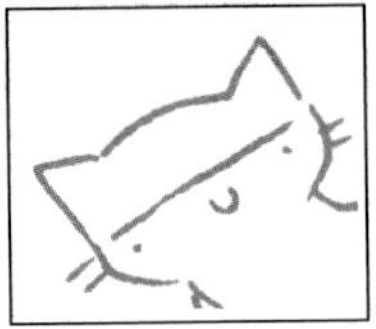

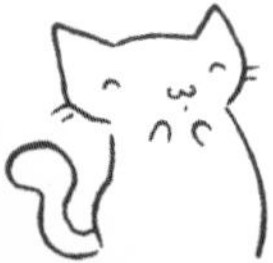

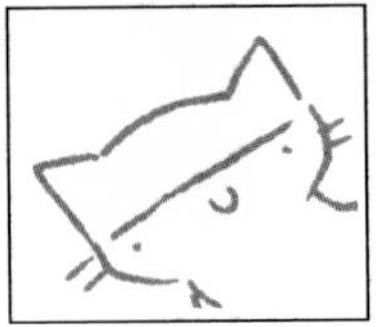

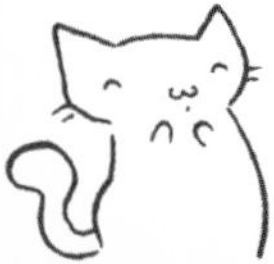